Further Education

★

essay

(as a symposium)

★

Traumear

*

An essay in the form of a symposium. Informal discussion of education mostly as chosen rather than as imposed, such as by the State. Education also viewed as not necessarily school education. A bridge from education by constraint to education by choice. The need of human beings to free themselves from prejudice and narrow-mindedness. Education that is 'further' also in the sense of ongoing. – Those who take part in the discussion are pupils, students, teachers and parents; also a banker, a philosopher, various scientists, a poet …

*

Further Education

Pupil A: I didn't give it much thought at first. I kind of slid into it. My O level marks were good, not very good, but all that meant was two more years of school, at the same school. Then my parents had a long talk with me.

Philosopher: Can you tell us what that was about?

Pupil A: It was complicated. My mother said one thing, my dad said another. I got the impression they were worried about something. But you expect parents to worry, don't you.

Philosopher: What did you think they were worried about?

Pupil A: Eventually it all boiled down to the fact that now I was at liberty to make up my own mind as to whether I should continue to go to school or not. My mother was concerned that I might decide not to go back, not to 'carry on with my education', as she called it. But I got the impression she was afraid of losing sight of me.

Philosopher: How do you mean, losing sight of you?

Pupil A: Well, if you can predict how a person is going to behave over the next few years, you feel more at ease about them. Most parents like to see their children settled in some predictable activity. My friends and I discussed that. We talked about how often we get asked some question equivalent to: What are you going to be when you grow up? Nowadays we get asked about our plans for the future. The look on the person's face is usually half scared and half hopeful, we decided. You don't like to disappoint an adult, because you never know about the consequences, so you prepare a few carefully crafted responses, such as: 'I'm looking into the possibility of trade and commerce,' or, if we want to close the subject before it opens too far: 'I only want to get on with my education for the time being.' For most adults the word 'education' is surrounded by a magical aura. They nod wisely and come over to your side.

Educational Psychologist: But what about your Dad? What did he have to say? Or better, what do you suppose was foremost in his mind?

Pupil: Yes, that's not necessarily the same thing, is it. Well, he made the point that the education would be different now. At first I didn't realize what he meant. In fact I'm still not quite sure what he meant. He said he would like it if, during the next few years, I learned how to decide to apply myself. He kept insisting that in his opinion that was the important thing for me to learn now. Then he said something like: 'If you can learn that at school, fine and dandy'. Well, I said, where else can I learn it? And he said: Anywhere at all. So I asked him was there any reason why I should go back to school and he said that school might very well be the best place for me to learn it.

Educationist: Excellent! That brings us nicely right into the middle of what I think we should talk about here. Would you mind very much if I just explored those two points you raised?

Pupil: Not at all.

Educationist: Thank you. Now I know you related an incident in your own life, but for me it sums up a general point of view. I wonder how many of the parents who came today will eventually agree with me. Youngsters around the age of sixteen have a disconcerting way of distancing themselves from their parents, don't they. Would I be stating it too strongly if I said that they judge us? They weigh our words. Don't we grownups weigh one another's words? Of course we do. One expects that. But our children for a while have unquestioningly believed everything we said to them. That made us feel good. It made us feel important. Convenient extensions of ourselves justified our opinions, our opinions of ourselves, too, and, dare I say, our prejudices. But now that disconcerting element intrudes. They can tell, for example, that there's a difference between what we feel and what we say. They may dimly have sensed that for years, but now the opportunity presents itself for exploitation.

Well, naturally, the biology can be discussed. The fledgling gets ready to leave the nest. The parent gets ready to push the fledgling out of the nest. Variations on that theme could fill books, but we might be smart to ask ourselves how much importance we really want to place on that biology, that so-called natural factor. One young man breaks up the furniture, slams the front door on his way out and isn't seen or heard of for ten years. Another one stays on in the parental home right through university and meanwhile his attitude and behaviour towards his parents undergoes many interesting and profound changes. In neither case has the biological law gone void or been deprived of its rights. In neither case has the fledgling remained in the nest too long. But wait a minute. If growing up means being able and willing to make up your own mind more frequently, then there is some likelihood that although our first youngster has stormed with finality out of the house, nevertheless the fledgling has not left the nest. For the next ten years he resents his parents and reacts to life rather than living it. The nest clings to him, like a straitjacket.

That's my way of emphasizing that we are dealing with human beings and not with birds. Mind you, for all I know crows have nervous breakdowns too. In any case, the facile image of a personal biology won't wash. If we want to make a good job of discussing secondary education, then the need to do justice to a specifically human reality, not to mention peculiarly human illusions, seems to me to be more crucial than ever.

A Parent: We found that with our first son. He probably has more in his head than the other two but he was never done inventing problems for everybody. I think he saw himself as a born trouble maker. And he liked himself in that role. It satisfied him. For a while we came up with nothing but the standard responses. You know, criticism, punishment. It was a habit, and we had turned it into a ritual, and it wore us all out. No more mutual respect, no affection, we were one sore family.

3

Then our second son was born, and Jack, the first one, started his secondary education. Suddenly there were no more problems. Why was that? We had totally lost interest in one another – he in us, we in him. In a sense we were relieved. For the next few years he only used the home for a house. He came and he went like a stranger, polite enough, but distant; and cynical. During those few years, right up to the time of his O levels, he must have worked something out for himself, because one day he came to us, asked us to sit down with him and out poured this great flood of self-recrimination. We were shocked. He told us how he hated himself for the way he'd got on, how sad he was that he really didn't know any more how to talk to us and that he was absolutely petrified at the prospect of doing A levels because he realized there was no way he could count on our moral support. We were floored. I think we were so ashamed, my wife and I, that we couldn't look at each other for a long time. Here he was telling us what we should have told him years go. And we could have, had we put our minds to it. Such a change has come over our family since then.

Philosopher: How absolutely amazing that you should confide in us like this! Personally I'm grateful. If you don't mind my saying so, your experience shows that the fledgling can't leave the nest unless he has first been properly in it.

Parent: Exactly.

A Girl: But what can you do if you only feel numb? I can hear you people congratulating each other but I don't understand what for. It only makes me angry. I've been going to school now faithfully for how long? Twelve years? And when I look back do you know how it strikes me? Like a great flowering of my youthful nature into adulthood, maybe? Or like a gradual accumulation of valuable skills and relevant information? No, but like a total waste of time! Worse than that, I consider it did me harm. I can honestly say that I haven't had a single good teacher – I mean a teacher who impressed me rather than nau-

4

seating me. Maybe I nauseate easy, but that's the fact. Not a single teacher I would turn to for advice today. It's all bland and bleak and monotonous. The high points, when I came closest to what I would call real experience, were when I was punished, physically. Some teachers who punished me – not all, mind you – seemed to care about <u>something</u> at least; though I could never exactly make out what it was. Self-consolation for a chronic sense of frustration, maybe? – I was told that if I showed up here this would be my chance to say exactly what I felt. I'm going to go ahead and say it, even though I suspect I'll probably regret having done so afterwards. I want to say that I hated some of my teachers so badly I could have murdered them. I think that inwardly I probably did. There now. That's one thing I learned to do at school. I learned to murder. Now my parents want me to keep going to school even though I don't have to, by law. I ask them: Why would I do that? I find their reasons too boring to mention. Well, you can tell that I haven't learned to mince my words. And I'm not going to go back to school. Not for my parents, not for the Minister of Education, especially not for my own good. I wouldn't recognize my own good if I fell over it. But when I've had my say now, that same stupor is going to descend on me, until the next time I get angry. That's the history of my adolescence, by the way. In a rage or drugged. I get so drugged that my tongue feels thick and sticks to the roof of my mouth. Does anybody here know what I mean? I doubt it. I mean drugged with boredom, monotony, self-disgust. I've never taken drugs in my life, by the way. But believe me, I don't condemn anybody who does.

A Parent: So what do you plan to do with yourself now? You can't just sit around and do nothing! From the sound of it your parents won't be too pleased with you in the house all day long. And I don't think you were born with the knack of living one day at a time.

5

Girl: There's nothing I want to do. I don't want to make any plans either. Do you know what I'd like? Do you want me to say, if I don't pretend, and if I'm totally honest, what I'd really prefer? To be dead. I'd like to be dead.

Philosopher: But the way you talk right now – you do that well. I'm glad I've listened to what you said.

Girl: That's because I'm upset. Do you think I like being upset? Do you want me to wait until something upsets me and then start to live?

Philosopher: Why not?

Girl: Besides, you don't really care about what I say except to the extent that it's grist for your mill. What are you, a psychologist?

Philosopher: Something like that.

Girl: Well, don't you find that it's true? Do you feel any compassion when you hear me rant and rave? I doubt it very much. You probably count your blessings that you don't have to face me in private. Other than that I probably fit in with your dogma or I don't. I either illustrate some intellectual conviction of yours or I don't. Beyond that, do you care for me? Do you love me? Don't make me laugh!

Philosopher: You do rather drive a hard bargain. But I take your point. If I knew what to say to you now I'd feel a whole lot better. Nevertheless, whatever has happened to you in the past, you can make a start. But you have to stop hating. And there's only one way to do that. If you can find that way, then it won't mater to you what your teachers did or didn't do or what your parents did or didn't do. If you can find that way, then you'll look forward and never look back again. Wondering why it was the way it was or how it might have been different. If you wish you were dead now, then you've an advantage over many people; they have to wait until they're much older before it comes to them as clear as that, and then it's much harder for them to decide, because the longer you wait, the more time was

6

wasted. Eventually everybody has to learn that their life doesn't depend on anything anyone out there can do for them, or to them for that matter. Some learn it early, some learn it late. I dare say most of us wait until we're staring into the grave. Why should you wait until then, if you can be free now?

A Teacher: I think it's nasty, preaching to a young girl at a time like this! Doesn't she have her whole life ahead of her? Shouldn't she have listened to her parents years ago?

A Teacher: Why should we teachers be made responsible for how a person turns out? School is for the intellect, not the soul. What has it got to do with education, secondary or otherwise, if a girl wishes she were dead? I feel sorry for her, but why are we here today?

Philosopher: Yes, we should really state our purpose again, especially for the sake of those who didn't attend our last symposium. Well, how should I put it this time! A-level education? How about: Education by choice, as compared to education by constraint? But we want to address ourselves specifically to the situation peculiar to young people who by law may quit school but may choose to continue with it.

Linguist: It's an interesting us of the word 'may', if I may interject at this point. First in the sense of 'allows', as: to be allowed, by law, to quit, and then in the sense of an opportunity presenting itself, as in the case of : They may or may not continue. The latter instance also reflects the uncertainty of the case. It kind of sums up what you have in mind, I think, and …

Philosopher: Please, let me finish. I agree with you about the uncertainly, by the way. But we have to set ourselves certain limitations. Last time, as some of you will remember, we thought about education and the system, about how teachers and pupils could best cope within that system. And we considered the attitudes of parents. So what exactly has changed now? For one thing, the child is a little older. For another, the child will soon leave home, which does not necessarily have to be a break in any sense of the word. And thirdly, the general pressure and stress due to legislation is to be replaced by the individual pupil's self-motivation, hopefully. So there's the biological factor, there is the cultural context, and finally we have the spiritual dimension. Naturally we cannot be expected to stick to categories like this, nor would we wish to, because it's the conversation we value, and the discoveries on the spot. Let's all be open-minded and tolerant of one another's points of view, please. But let's also try to return to our main theme, if we find ourselves straying too far. That can be achieved in all sorts of subtle, diplomatic ways.

A Parent: I wonder if I could just set the tone a little. Are we going to turn this into a binge of problem-detection and problem-solving? I sincerely hope not. There's a normal way of growing up, of going to school and university, or to school and a job. There's also a normal way of leaving the home, getting married and creating one's own home. By normal I don't mean a method or a recipe, but generally the way things go. Not that there aren't any problems, but as soon as they crop up they get solved. I want to emphasize at the outset here that a happy progress in life within a harmonious environment exists within the realm of possibility, even for teenagers. It's not necessarily a series of traumata, of delinquencies and breakdowns. I'm quite aware, buy the way, that an emotionally repressed juvenile delinquent will probably not be sustained much by being told to be normal, although even there it would depend a great deal on who says it, and why. But this notion of normality is very dear to me. I mean, I myself just now mentioned going to school and university, or to school and a job, and to a complete outsider from mankind it sounds for all the world as if those were the two available channels of being and behaviour for a young human being. Of course that's absurd. It's conceivably possible for a human being not to go to school, not to have a job and not go to university and lead a perfectly normal life. We may have

8

a little difficulty picturing that as occurring in our own back yard, but how about in Baluchistan; or in France two hundred years from now? Who can say, right? I'm not proposing a far-fetched line of discussion here; quite on the contrary. I want to make sure that we look at our own nearest and dearest interests from several points of view, and in perspective. Both the formal education and the paid job are more or less customary forms of existence, neither necessary nor perfectly optional ways of life. Unless we want to risk maybe ending up talking in circles, we might be wise to consider that a great number of so-called problems are only aggravated, and aberrations are created, by a stubborn failure to recognize fundamental priorities; by a wilful insistence on putting the cart before the horse and then maybe shooting the horse because it refuses to be pulled by the cart. Education, a job, a career – they're only three out of a thousand possibilities. Wouldn't it be terrible for anybody to lose sight of that? Imagine being crippled by one's own ideas and thoughts!

A Young Person: I welcome that. It gives me a lot to think about. It explains to me why I don't feel happy with any degree of pressure on me. Not that I can't cope with pressure, but I don't understand the reason for it in the first place. I think I suspect that I'm probably responsible for it myself, on account of a blind spot somewhere, a false assumption, about existence maybe, like you said. I took a year off from school and I intend to go to university eventually, but first I want to be quite certain in myself that the choice is my own. One thing I've discovered: a true choice takes more time and consideration than an accident. And I am really and truly sick and tired of accidents. That's how I view my education until now, one long series of accidents. Some were fortunate enough, but that's not the point. I've decided that next time I speak to a teacher, to a lecturer or a professor of any knowledge at all, I'll be able to respect him, on an equal footing with myself. I'll know that I have as much to offer to him as he to me, and I won't resent him if he doesn't know that or if he refuses to believe it.

A parent: Whatever do you mean? How can you have as much to offer to a teacher as he to you?

Young Person: It's a two-way traffic. Here we talk about education of the voluntary sort now. There's a vast difference between going to school by one's own personal choice and going to school for any other conceivable reason such as because the law says you must, or to please your parents, or so that you can stay with your friends, or because you're afraid for your livelihood; and then there is the prestige factor too.

Philosopher: Wait a moment. Let me play devil's advocate. Can somebody not personally choose to go back to school so that one day he can lord it over the rest of us?

Young Person: I may be putting too fine a point on it, but technically no. Now that's the way I feel about it, right now; I'm not saying that one day I won't change my individuality, or that eventually I won't arrive at a more mature insight. I'm only seventeen years old. But my contention is, that a truly personal choice has to be made for a universal reason. And reasons like that can't be stated in so many words. I've had occasion to ask around. Most of those who say they know exactly why they want to go back to school don't convince me. Especially not if they have their reason down pat. I tend to believe those more who make something up on the spot. An maybe next time they're asked they make something else up. That ties in with what the person who spoke before me said. It has to do with not confusing means with ends. A truly personal choice is not built on reasons but the reasons come afterwards, like decoration for the cake. The way we choose is the way we live – if we do it well. It's not the way we plan and calculate, which is usually based on fear anyway, or on greed. It's like when somebody says he's happy, he's not really happy if some challenge, like criticism, makes him sad.

10

A Minister of the Church: I find it extraordinary that words like that should be spoken by a seventeen-year-old. Our education system couldn't be as bad as it's cracked up to be.

Young Person: Why do you say that? If you mean it as a compliment, then it might just as readily be the case that I've had a proper upbringing or that I'm exceptionally clever. Or maybe you were being sarcastic. Do you say I'm precocious? And does that amuse you?

The Minster of the Church: No, no. Good heavens! Not at all.

A Teacher: That highlights a very real and personal problem in my profession. I wonder if this might not be a good time to bring it up. I've only recently begun to teach advanced level courses, and I have to admit it's more of a challenge than I expected. You'll have to bear with me, if you would, please, because I haven't tried to put this into words before, and also because I'd like to trust everybody here so that I can confess a bit. You see, my first impression was: Hurray, the pressure is off, now I can relax, because if they didn't want to learn they wouldn't be here. But that was wide of the mark on every count. The pressure isn't off. It's only a different pressure. It's more internal now. The interesting thing is that my pupils describe it generally in the same way. I was in the same boat with them when I taught the first five forms, and I'm in the same boat with them now. I think first it was a rowboat and now it's a sailboat. Then it was the law of the land, now it's volition. But it's not as if they all wanted to learn either. It's nowhere near as simple as that, is it. There are all those reasons for coming back to school that this young man mentioned, and a few more besides. And I don't feel entirely comfortable with the suggestion some of my colleagues make, that if they don't want to learn, it's not my job to encourage them. So I try to leave them to it for a while, and then I prod them, but that's not working too well so far. Also, when I ask them if they want to learn, a little voice in me sniggers, as if to say: learn what? As if to say: Are you so confident that you have something worthwhile to teach? And if you indulge in doubts like this, should you not maybe look for another way of making a living? But then I think: well, perhaps I can help them make the sort of real personal choices that signify the mature human being. And then I realize that first of all I have to be able and willing to make them myself. And that's really the main part of my job right now, would you believe it? For all I know that will always be the main part. It might make sense. After all, with the kind of choices we have in mind here, it's no help at all if somebody from behind a proverbial counter preaches a catechism to you or comes up with a lot of standards for you to salute or abide by. The only thing that makes the crucial difference, so far as I can make out, is the genuine individual example. But how can a teacher set that sort of example unless time and again she has cause to do so? And what is a sufficient cause? Should I tell you how it appears to me? I have never said this to anyone. My opinion is that the only cause sufficient for an exemplary personal choice is an experience of spiritual insecurity.

A Poet: Now wait a moment. I've got to butt in here. There's only so much any person can do. There's only so much any person should try to do. You sound to me like you're getting ready to sacrifice yourself for your pupils. That really isn't necessary. There's so much going on in each one of us, you know! We real don't need anybody's sacrifice. Besides, what good can it do? You condemn yourself to repeated spiritual insecurity so that you can demonstrate again and again – what? – the heroic choice? The free choice in spite of overwhelming hindrance? Really now, come along. Are you not maybe forgetting the one single element that crops up in each and ever adolescent sooner or later, and there's nothing you can do to make it happen, but without it you haven't a hope of any personal initiative?

Philosopher: Well, go ahead now, you've started us in a new directions. What is that element?

The Poet: Why, it's quite simply the thing we call adolescence! It's the acquisition of a taste for spiritual sweetness.

A Teacher: What!

The Poet: I can see I am going to get myself into trouble here, but let's face it, that's the name of the game. I'm going to say it again, exactly the way I said it the first time, because I want to rub it in, not just to make myself obnoxious: adolescence is the acquisition of a taste for spiritual sweetness. Is that such a revolutionary statement, I wonder? Does it imply certain risks? Do I detect a hint of tragedy? – Now don't tell me that nobody here has seen it flit past him, if not years ago, then perhaps just now when I mentioned it. It comes quick and moves off again quick, adolescence does, and happy is the one who captures it. That's where the teacher should apply his wits, in my opinion, when a child comes back to school even when he doesn't have to. – Let's just for a moment assume that there really is such a thing as adolescence quite separate and apart from a certain age of a number of years, you know – the teen age, the between age. Wouldn't it be marvellous if a youngster could get just precisely the specific kind of help he needs at that point in his experience! Why should he have to surround himself with a culture all his own – not that it isn't a great deal of an improvement on no culture at all. But why does he have to immerse himself in that test tube of a pop culture, in that laboratory of the teen-scene? It's because we so-called grown-ups are letting him down, that's why. We're afraid of the teen-ager's adolescence, for all sorts of good reasons, such as we missed or spoiled our own adolescence, because we didn't get any help either but only judgment and repression – or because we just plain can't be bothered trying to be compassionate where pity isn't involved and where the person in front of us may well have more on the ball than we do. I've lived in America, where we like to try things out. – Let me emphasize what I mean and strongly believe: Teachers are afraid of the adolescence of their pupils. And the sad thing is, there's no need for it, because all one needs, to be able to deal quite safely and constructively – an humanly, let me add – with anyone's adolescence, is trust. Trust is the thing. And it's unconditional trust. Not "I trust you if you can first prove to me that you're trustworthy" but "I trust you so that we have that only legitimate and workable basis for getting on with what we're here to do. I don't care so much whether or not <u>you</u> trust <u>me</u>, that isn't really my business. After all, <u>I'm</u> supposed to be the grownup, the parent or the teacher. And if nobody trusted <u>me</u> when I needed it most, during my adolescence, then let me get on with it myself all the more, because I know what it's like to miss it, and to resent having to go without it, and to rage because instead of having food, I end up consuming my<u>self</u>."

Philosopher: Now we're getting somewhere. These are specifics. I wonder how many teachers of teenage pupils are of the opinion that their charges present them with unique and wonderful opportunities. What did you call it, sir? A taste for spiritual sweetness? I must say!

A Teacher: There's no doubt that more than enough teenagers give me the impression that they're a different breed altogether. But we usually only mention the unpleasant aspects of their difference, don't we. I was that glad when I'd made it through my own teens without too much disaster. Many parents breathe a sigh of relief – or they cut their losses. It would be an improvement of course if one knew a little bit what to expect.

A Girl: You can say that again! I sincerely wish I knew what to expect.

The Poet: Well does that make any sense to you, what I said? That at a certain age it's as if something novel were being injected into the biology of a young person. Should we call it youth? And would you not like to contemplate the possibility of calling it good?

A Parent: That's a poet's business, isn't it; to praise what should be praised but for one reason or another people have downgraded it and allowed it to depreciate.

A Girl: It's not the sort of thing I can make up my mind about on the spot. When you've been told all your life to be like everybody else you don't take kindly to any originality or novelty in your system. I mean if my parents had told me between the age of seven and twelve that sooner or later I will feel the hand of god on me – and that god is good – I would very probably have looked forward more eagerly to what eventually only confused me.

Poet: You see, we shouldn't be afraid to look at everything afresh. A lot of my own views on adolescence sound odd for only that one reason, that they don't fit in with most people's views on childhood. If during childhood you weren't prepared for adolescence, then adolescence has to appear like an ogre – or one will simply wish it away and lo and behold it never arrives. How often do you hear it said about someone? He behaves like an eternal adolescent. And that is meant pejoratively. What a shame! The person who never grows up and is, say, sexually promiscuous through his twenties and thirties, is described as adolescent, with the implication that adolescence along with other aberrations, means sexual promiscuity. That's a terrible injustice. Why not take me seriously when I say that adolescence is the development of a taste for spiritual sweetness, and that sexual promiscuity is a regrettable waste of time. You can waste your time any time, but adolescence only comes once. If you miss it then you may never get another chance. And if, instead of developing that taste, you corrupt it, or repress it, or neglect it, is it any wonder that for the years to come you will suffer the damage of it?

Sociologist: And would you not say that our own time has its own adolescence-related hang-ups and risks?

Poet: Certainly. What I say about adolescence goes for all time but our contemporary age has its own characteristic way of manifesting symptoms of error in that realm of experience. When I say: 'taste for spiritual sweetness' I calculate my expression to fit the times. Spirit and reality are for me almost interchangeable. Teenagers are confronted, often with singular vehemence, by the problem of what is real. The notion of a personal god ties very much into that. And that reality, or the spirit, should introduce itself sweetly – I mean rather than reasonably, or morally, or politically – this should interest the contemporary physiologist in every creative human being to the point of excitement. This is what makes of adolescence the issue of our day. Consequently we have very good reason for looking to thwarted adolescence for an explanation of such monstrosities as frustrated sexuality and a system of rewards for cynical realism and embittered resentment.

A Parent: You go too far. I can't follow that.

A Teacher: Yes, it's time we returned to the major theme of our discussion, don't you feel? Voluntary secondary education. I can't honestly say that I've learned much from this digression into the nature of the adolescent. In my own experience these so-called Advanced Level pupils are a year or two older, that's all. If you teach them during the previous five years you really don't notice a change. They're not suddenly students.

Philosopher: Of courses it doesn't happen suddenly. But I'm interested by your use of the word student.

Educationist: Yes, and surely what counts is what a teacher has in mind when he approaches a pupil as compared to what he has in mind when he has to do with a student. And an adolescent should in fact be educated from a specific point of view, I feel very strongly about that.

A Psychologist: There is puberty and there is adolescence. I see them as two sides of the same coin. If we still agree, from our previous conversations, that education, if it deserves the name, is of human beings and not only of minds or intellects, then we can hardly fail to see the importance of taking adolescence and puberty into account. There is adolescent aggression and the dream of puberty side by side, not to be ignored with impunity. There's the necessity of free choice, if I may put it that way; and all the ingenious attempts to wriggle out of it. On the other hand there is the opportunity of free choice and all the callous attempts to abuse it.

An Adolescent: Do you ever ask adolescents how they feel about it?

A Parent: I really don't think that would be realistic. Feel about what? The sort of education that would be best for them? It's a topic entirely for grownups. If <u>we</u> can't come up with what you need, nobody can.

A Teacher: I happen to agree with that. When it comes to development towards adulthood, let's talk <u>about</u> teenagers, but let's not talk <u>to</u> them. It confuses them if we show them our methods and reveal to them our reasons for what we do for them. As a matter of fact, there shouldn't be an adolescents at this symposium.

A Parent: Quite right. Between parents and children a distance should be preserved. Also between teachers and pupils, or between teachers and students, if you want to keep that distinction on hand. A sure way to not bring a child up is by being childish. Personally I always end up regretting it. Grownups have a way of regressing when they spend time with young people. This is a delicate subject. I certainly don't mean to exclude friendship; on the contrary.

A Parent: No. Actually friendship isn't possible either if we let down our hair too often. But then that's not the right expression. Of course we should be able to relax and have fun with our children. I think if comes down to this: To what extent are we ourselves grown up. And finally I have to say: I don't think anybody is ever completely grown up, or let's put it this way: completely incapable of being childish.

Philosopher: So doesn't that particular little insight prompt us to invite adolescents back into this symposium?

A Teacher: How so?

Philosopher: If it's true, as I do believe, by the way, that it is – that every grownup has it in him to regress and be childish, then isn't it equally true that every adolescent – perhaps every child – has it in him to suddenly be quite grown up for a while? And wouldn't that dual insight, if I may call it that, encourage and justify us in expecting some extremely enlightening exchanges – I mean, between grownup parents and teachers who acknowledge their tendency to regress and adolescents who are willing to exercise their ability to understand and be wise.

Sociologist: You may just have come up with the only way to bridge the generation gap. I like it. Do you mind if I quote you in my forthcoming book?

Philosopher: Not at all. But I'd like to hear some opinions on this. It occurred to me only just now, in that particular formulation

Psychologist? Let me add something to it that seems to me to follow from it quite naturally. The generation gap is an unpleasant and often painful fact. Let's not waste any time asking what causes it or how it comes about. There must be as many reasons as there are possibilities of human error. Let's instead concentrate precisely on such a measure, such a disposition as you just mentioned, to overcome it. But better than that. I feel that the very existence of such a generation gap, once identified in any particular instance, constitutes the best possible opportunity for adolescence education, especially at the voluntary stage. If grownups respond to that generation gap by acknowledging their tendency to be childish, which is essentially a response of modesty, then adolescence education is very fundamentally served. Young people find it nearly impossible not to respond, then, to that modest acknowledgment. And when they do respond, it's a case of sensibility, and of receptivity, and perhaps of a great deal more.

A Parent: When I was eighteen I learned nothing at school that helped me cope with my personal grievances. My parents began to talk in a different language. I saw through them. My teachers went by the book. It wasn't until I went to jail that I had the good fortune to met somebody who, in my opinion at the time, knew what he was talking about. I mean that literally. While he talked, his knower was switched on. He helped me make sense of my past. That was the real education for me. Twice a week he visited me and we talked for an hour. It was worth going to jail for that. I tell my own youngsters today to think for themselves. To feel for themselves. The generation gap: What is that? Show me the equivalent in 'Hamlet', or in 'Macbeth'. What about 'Middlemarch', 'The Ambassadors', 'The Waves'? Literary criticism is no fit occupation for a teen-ager. I started to read books in prison. Repeatedly I asked my-self: Why wasn't this presented to me when I needed it most! Most of the so-called adults who taught me at school, and who called themselves teachers, had opted out themselves when they were sixteen, to join the rat race. What they called adult-hood was a case of grudging resignation to small pleasures and the need to survive. In no way did that appeal to me, so I drank and stole cars and got into fights. And do you know what? In a sense I'm glad I did. And I say that knowing that my own son is listening to me. The alternative, for me, at that time, well, it doesn't bear thinking about. I was restless. I was lonely and I was bored, and I was told that was a bad thing. Sex in those days wasn't talked about. Nothing has changed. Today its talked about. I had to go to prison to learn that youth is a good thing if you don't waste it. Happily I was able to catch up. I honestly can't see how any young person, especially once he's free to make a few choices, can properly get anywhere unless he first learns how to impose discipline on himself. He should learn how to put himself behind lock and key, for sizeable periods of time, this should be stressed by those adults around him who have learned from experience that it's true. I would tell anyone who wants to grow up: Don't try to survive but find out how to live. Your fist voluntary decision may have to be to deny yourself. If you wait until others do it for you, it takes twice as long and its twice as tricky for you to come around to it yourself afterwards.

A Parent: You are talking about a minority. Two or three out of a hundred. Open up special schools for them by all means. I grant you, they are worth it. Just the same as you were worth it. Let's stop pretending that the average school kid wants to develop his soul. He wouldn't know what one looked like.

A Parent: All the more reason to point it out to him, surely?

A parent: That's pious crap. Nobody believes in souls today. Matter is what matters. I agree with the percentage estimate: Two out of a hundred, and I side with the ninety-eight every time. What we need today is managers with a sense of commitment, engineers who can talk to their wives, technicians who can keep their collective noses to the grindstone. Not spiritualists. Not people who tell us we don't die, so what's all the fuss about sex and comfort. I'm glad that somebody can go to prison and learn something from the experience but let's not generalise.

A Geologist: (also a teacher of geology) I teach Geology. I don't have time to fool around in the classroom. And I don't decide on the spot what to teach. The curriculum is laid out. But I can tell when a youngster shows a little interest. I encourage that, but I have to wait for it. I don't believe in trying to whip up enthusiasm for rocks. And I certainly wouldn't be minding my business if I tried to whip up enthusiasm for anything else. What's a classroom? It's like a human laboratory. Those pupils who choose to be in a classroom rather than somewhere else are not looking for inspiration, or for morality, or for a closer relationship with their god. There are places for that, and there are times for that. Some great poets failed Geology and Physics. They even failed Literature. School is no place for learning how to be creative. If somebody wants to develop his original individuality let him do it in spite of school. Voluntary secondary education is bound to be relevant exclusively for those who have been brought up already – and incidentally for those who will probably never grow up. Let's not waste time over which group we'd like to see in the majority. But we might keep in mind that those who are grown up – or nearly grown up – won't mistake a classroom for the space where their inner life is located. I used to teach ten- and eleven-year-olds. That's a different story altogether. Mind you, something is to be said for those two years we call A level education as intermediary between what comes before it and the university education that very likely comes after it. To be not quite grown up and to go to university is a fatal mistake, in my opinion. If we don't know for certain at university whether we have an inner life or not, then we'll probably end up not caring whether we do or not. Again, that's not the fault of the university. I have certain fixed opinions about the specific uses of a university education; I won't divulge my weaknesses at this moment.

Philosopher: But you equate growing up with the awareness of a developing inner life?

Geologist: Well, that's one way of putting it. I was brought up; by my parents and incidentally by one or two teachers. During that time I learned to differentiate between appearances and reality. I learned to appreciate appearance, but to value reality. And I became convinced that the way to reality every day is appearance. And the way to the truth, every time one goes that way, is illusion. You know the old adage: 'Nobody can come to the Father except by way of the Son,.' Once I realized that, I decided I was grown up. That's when I also decided to be a teacher, at least for some part of my life.

Philosopher: But what do you teach – is it appearance? Is it illusion?

Geology Teacher: Certainly. Very important appearance, and very useful illusion. I don't teach ends, but means. That's why I'm ever so relaxed in my work. Some of my colleagues envy me.

Philosopher: So if Geology is a means, what is the end?

Geologist: That's entirely up to the pupil, and to the student. I think of them as pupils during sixth lower and as students during sixth upper. That serves me personally as an invaluable guideline.

Educational Psychologist: but tell us, do you hold that everything except the inner life is appearance and illusion?

Geologist: These are strange questions but yes, it's a stage, in my opinion, and everybody who wants to amount to something – or to someone – has to go through it. The inner life is bound to reveal itself as so strong, and primary, that 'everything outside' is bound to seem illusive. But then comes the contribution of the human being, so that illusions are made concrete and appearance is realized, and I see that as happening, or rather as being done, more and more as the student comes to the end of his career as student. Once he becomes active, with full authority of his own – but really this belongs elsewhere, and we shouldn't discuss it at all here. I only mention it to show how I view the development of the student. He studies appearance and illusion – appearances and illusions. And he knows better every day what good reason he has for doing so, because of his inner life.

Mathematics Teacher: This sounds like a kind of model you've sketched out for us. I think I might find that helpful. Do you not sit down sometimes after your day of being a teacher is over and wonder where you've gone wrong? It's at times like that, especially when I can't see how I've been effective during the day, that I miss the bone structure for my profession, or call it the physical foundation. Let's face it, most of what we teach is mental, and intellectual. Even you, with your rocks; they sound tangible enough, but you don't build with them. You analyze them, and speculate about them, where they come from, what sort of evidence they make. That's mental. But our other half is our body, and often I wonder how it gets so regrettably left out of the picture. And how we don't keel over, so overloaded to one side of our human nature. Now when you come along with your model of the student, that helps me reflect. And it gives me something permanent to reflect on, don't you see. Studying appearances and illusions for the sake of the inner life, you say. And eventually it spills over, this inner life, is that how you might see it? And then we don't study illusions so much as we create realities. I sense a very productive line of thought here. My own field is mathematics, by the way. The differential calculus thrills me no end, but I wish I could pass some of that excitement on to my students more frequently. They sit there and look at me, almost a if I had promised them something but now I wasn't keeping my promise. "Calculus will be a friend to you for life," I tell them, but I'm not wholly sure they believe me. Still, they come to class, they take notes – and I go home feeling I haven't quite delivered the goods. It's an experience I don't relish and I have it more frequently as I get on in life. Now I look at that model of yours and suddenly I ask myself: Am I not content enough, or not realistic enough, to teach appearances, while maybe at the same time, and for complementary reasons, I don't leave enough up to the pupils themselves? Maybe I overlook, for example, that it takes time for them to digest and assimilate, and that I really don't have a right to expect any evidence of the fact that I succeed as a teacher. Could be what holds me back is a secret desire to have them come to me and thank me for changing their lives for the better. Right now I can't imagine anything sillier, but that doesn't mean that I'm entirely free from it.

Sociologist: Right now I'd like to know how anybody can teach Geology or Mathematics for any other reason except more Geology and more mathematics. Or maybe I misunderstand your model. If it's true that you teach appearances and illusions, how can that lead to anything other than more appearances and more illusions?

Geologist: It <u>can</u> do only if the pupils or the students are grown up, or nearly grown up. They've got to be able to assimilate stuff, like my colleague suggested. I use the word stuff advisedly. They have to be aware of the fact that what we observe as outside of ourselves needs some contribution from inside ourselves before it can make proper sense. They have to have some education under their belts, in other words. They should be able to select and to comprehend. Some of them are in fact able to do that. They're the more important ones within the framework of further education, because they want to continue their studies. My so-called model pertains to them.

A Parent: But what about the rest!

Geologist: You can't teach everybody everything all the time. I must insist, for my own peace of mind even if no one else believes me, that only those who have nearly grown up should tackle further education. That starts with advanced level grammar school, or at some equivalent stage in any other system. If we don't have a firm notion in our mind of what it means to grow up, and to be brought up, our thoughts about further education are bound to miss the mark. I fully realize that this symposium was set up in the name of further education. I do concern myself with that. It's of vital importance – if we don't want to get caught up in bad ambitions, in misguided hopes – that in the case of further education, generally now, we differentiate between <u>skill</u> and <u>character</u>. It doesn't really apply to the child up to puberty. But the adolescent demands that distinction. Nobody can do justice to the adolescent nature, whether in terms of behaviour or with respect to development, unless he is willing to honour the character of that person, while at the same time offering scope to the cultivation of relevant skills. If you ask me: What about those who at the age of sixteen still haven't an inkling of character, nor of any capacity for skills, then all I can say is: They should definitely not go into further education. That doesn't mean I reject them, but we have to draw the circumference for this symposium somewhere. I don't wish to be misunderstood about what I mean by skills either. There are <u>manual skills</u>, <u>physical skills</u>, and <u>spiritual skills</u>. They are all of equal importance, of equal value. Those who perform them have reason and cause to amply exactly the same standards, I mean such as <u>conscientiousness, ethics and morality</u>, and <u>mastery</u>.

A Teacher: You must be joking!

Geologist: I certainly am not joking. The electrician performs a skill, so does the geologist, and so does the poet. I realize that there is more to it than that, but we want to confine ourselves here to education, and I would consciously limit education, I mean further education, to the cultivation of skills in relation to character. I think it's a grave mistake to expect more from further education than this cultivation of skills, but we go equally wrong if we neglect to relate the development of skills to maturing and mature individuals. The mere development of skills is a farce. It's essentially a farce and effectively a curse. Cultivated skills, by comparison, however common or subliminal, are nurtured in the disposition of the performer and they spring from his organic being. The have meaning to him, as working extensions of himself, as sources of vitality both for himself and for others. Viewed in that particular light, the parity becomes obvious, of the plumber's skill with his blowtorch, colder and flux, the surgeon's skill with his scalpel, needle and thread, and the poet's skill with his pen, paper and ink, or his speech, his voice and his words.

A Teacher: Surely there must be a qualitative and quantitative difference between the skill of a seamstress and the skill of a surgeon!

Geologist: When a surgeon-to-be studies anatomy it's not so that he can contemplate the comparative beauties of the liver and the spleen. It's so that he knows where to cut. He also becomes a diagnostician; but not so that he can stand back and reflect on the decay of your immune system, but so that he can decide competently when to cut, and whether or not to cut. Do you see what I'm getting at? Skill has to do with matter and with material. By the same token it also has to do with instruments and tools, among which have to be included the use of our hands, legs tongue and vocal chords as instruments and tools. Skills are performed in space and time, right here and now, and in the light of day. What I mean to most definitely exclude are the three Ms, if you don't mind my mentioning masturbation, magic and mysticism. Or call them self-gratification, self-aggrandizement and self-glorification. I don't want to raise a storm of contention here, only to emphasize what I mean by real skills. Further education, in my considered opinion, is a down-to-earth business. Everything that smacks of spiritualism, that is to say of the avoidance and negation of matter, is to be shunned.

Neither of course do we want mere skills. Who can come to terms satisfactorily with the crucial difference between matter and the flesh? By mere skill I mean the demonic, the fiendish element. We are all prone to it, composers, accountants and housewives alike. But this particular failing we can't shun and we can't avoid, because we either fail or else we succeed in the opposite direction, and that's the direction of human character, which has to be consciously chosen. We don't happen into it through mere wishful thinking, and in order to choose it, and to persevere in it, we have to reject and overcome a great mass of contrary tendencies and popular constraints.

Here we come back to the other half, or let's call it the stronger, or better part, of further education, which is the relation of real skills to the actual human character of pupils and students. And as usual, the stronger part is the more hidden part. It's tacit, not stated. It encompasses everything the good teacher keeps in mind and reflects on in person while he teaches. It dictates his attitude towards the information he imparts and it shapes his emotion and temperament in view of the skills he transmits. It informs his reason and purpose for instilling those skills and throws light, often with alarming intensity, on his reason for considering those skills worthy of attainment in the first place.

Philosopher: Why don't you illustrate what you mean. Perhaps you might have recourse to particular subjects on the average school curriculum. Such as Mathematics, Literature, Art, Religious Studies.

Geologist: I'm not sure we should get into that. Human character is a complicated business. It depends too much on the particular case, I would think, to bear scrutiny at a casual forum like this.

A Parent: The discussion is getting too technical in any case. I'm getting a headache. We should take a couple of hours for lunch and a long walk. I can recommend the stroll around the lake, also a boat ride.

A Teacher: I would have just liked to hear how anybody can consciously choose human character over spiritualism and the demonic. I mean does one do that one morning over breakfast or what!

Geologist: Any time and any where is a good time and place for it. First, of course, we have to realize that the choice exists. What I mean by human character is the way someone stands up to you and says: I have my own way of looking at that. If you expect me to learn something from you, you will have to help me overcome my reluctance to learn, and the best way to do that is simply to acknowledge that you suffer from that same reluctance. Or a teacher with character will say: Don't expect me to make everything palatable for you. I can only tell you how I see things from my own point of view but that won't make much useful sense to you unless you test yourself against it. If you swallow it unchewed you are bound to get stomach ache.

Philosopher: Aha! So character, for you, is something like recognition of one's own personal being. But that won't wash. because we have to agree on a common ground. We have to be able to take a tradition for granted. On the basis of that tradition we communicate. When it breaks down, we ... well, we ...

Geologist: Fall back on our character, if we have any; precisely. It's nothing magical. On the contrary. A great way to build up character is to hold out against magic. Character refuses to be overruled, or to be outwitted. So when we have even a morsel of character, we don't have to worry about whether or not some charismatic figure in front of us gives himself airs, and if somebody tells us we're wrong, that doesn't right away mean that we have to justify ourselves, in public or in private, and we won't worry about keeping the upper hand, or about being seen to do so. A person with character can keep his mouth shut without fading into insignificance and he can stand up for himself without becoming abusive, or self-defensive.

A Teacher: And you still maintain that we show the first signs of character in our adolescence?

Geologist: I do indeed. It comes along with youth; the capacity for character. And depending on how well the child was raised, the youth will recognize in himself this new appetite, and those around him won't mistake it.

A Parent: Has it got anything to do with consciousness? Or with self-consciousness?

Geologist: I really don't think so. With self-awareness, maybe. Isn't it the time when we become aware of the fact that we make a difference to those around us? The very fact that we exist makes a difference, we don't even have to say or do anything. And then it's the way that young fellow in the Book of Job puts it, after all the old men failed with their traditional wisdom: "It is a spirit in man, the breath of the Almighty, that gives him understanding. It is not those of many days who are wise, nor the aged who understand the right. Therefore I say: Hearken to me." And he had kept his peace until he was fit to burst. So it's a sign of adolescence, likewise, that we find we have something to say. What happens if nobody is willing to listen? I call it introversion. Or even inversion. That's the opposite to character. A cultural blindness sets in – and it's cultivated. After a time, if you mention the word spirit to such an individual, the best you can hope for is a hollow laugh.

Educational Psychologist: But the seeds for adolescence are sown before puberty comes along, surely. We shouldn't expect too much clear-cut evidence of essential adolescence in too many of our sons and daughters, and pupils, if we haven't brought them up patiently to that awareness of their inner life, to a familiarity with it, so that when something happens there and when somebody arrives there they aren't bowled over.

A Parent: I still say we should make a break. I can't cope with any more. What's the use of you people continuing with your discussion if I can't follow it? I need to eat. To have a rest and a change of scenery. Please!

Geologist: Of course. I apologize. I hate to get carried away like this. It does nobody any good. But we've at long last come around to viewing adolescence in a positive light. When we come back we should be able to have another look at this notion of skill and character, and I don't actually see why it shouldn't be possible to analyze a particular curriculum subject, such as mathematics, in terms of it.

*

We felt marvellously elated when we got outside. It was a relief not to have to think for a while. Also, the weather had turned. A light drizzle that morning had freshened everything up and now the sun beamed down, surprisingly warm for October. The campus was nearly deserted. A few students sat chatting on benches or were making their way to the cafeteria, the one next door to the library, behind those two great holm oaks that have looked down favourably on the comings and goings of so many generations of young people in the pursuit of degrees and knowledge. The red brick façade of the Students Union building peered through between several pines that had nearly reached maturity.

A couple beside me commented on the incredibly blue sky. I pointed to the sea gulls competing for scraps and then rushing off in pursuit of one another between the trees and over the rooftops.

I ended up at the same table with several individuals, one of them a flamboyant lady with red hair, who, during the course of the lunch claimed descent from a royal family on some West Indian island. She dropped her tray on the floor, later she spilled her water, and finally she ripped her tights on a tack sticking out of her chair. We sympathized very time. Her daughter wanted to go to college but her husband insisted on early marriage for the girl. Next to her sat a couple who spoke very little and held hands under the table. I would have liked to find out more about them, but I got the impression they were frightened of me, so I curbed my curiosity and concentrated my attention on my food until a man in a yellow shirt, directly opposite me, addressed me in person:

"We have too much on our minds, eh? What do you thing?"

"How do you mean?" I raised eyebrows – smiled.

"Do you have children of your own? I have four. I never spoke once in there. I couldn't. I wouldn't have known what to say. I feel surrounded by experts and professionals. They overawe me, do you know what I mean? I'm not exactly satisfied with the progress we've made. It's called a symposium, but how many of us parents really came out with anything relevant? It's as if we don't count. Most of the discussion went over my head, I'll be totally honest about that."

Before I could reply, a person to my immediate right spoke up with unexpected vehemence:

"Then you should fight for a hearing. No use complaining afterwards."

I turned and looked into the flushed face of a strikingly attractive young woman. The challenge in her voice had been unmistakable.

"No, I mean it," she went on, evidently unwilling to be put off by polite smiles. "I hate myself for not being able to command a particular point of view, but it's my own fault. I didn't enjoy myself this morning, I only felt ignorant. But I got something out of it. I listened. Maybe this afternoon I can make a bit more sense of it. Don't get me wrong, if you hadn't complained, I probably would have."

"That's what was wrong," I interjected, with an attempt at levity. "There were no contentious issues. Maybe we have to be able to argue, against something, before the old intelligence is stirred.

"Nonsense! You are totally in the wrong!" somebody shouted from my left, and nearly everybody laughed.

A man who looked like a banker spoke in a remarkably quiet voice after this, slowly and deliberately: "Isn't it true that so much of what goes on between us and our teenage children is consigned by us often rather fearfully to the realm of painful privacy. Outwardly we pay lip service to the standard current opinions while inwardly we draw the bolt across because we don't know what goes on, we're afraid of what might be demanded of us, and it doesn't particularly bolster our self-esteem when we're forced to admit how often we'd prefer to

31

wash our hands of the whole business by ignoring personal relations here and now in favour of cut and dried conventional plans for some totally predictable future."

"Ah yes, personal relations!" the man in the yellow shirt sighed. "And in a family, too. It's come around to that, hasn't it. Everything nowadays needs to be dissected. If it isn't analyzed it falls apart."

"You sound like you speak from experience."

"And mostly bad. I lost my family. I'm trying to understand in retrospect. Before my marriage broke up I tinkered with it, but to no avail. The despair at the core of it grew like a cancer. I was too busy making money, the old story. But you know something? Since then I've come to suspect even my motives for doing the so-called providing. I'm astonished that I can say this here. I believe I became such a diligent provider because I was incapable of personal intimacy. My precious work became a convenient barrier between my self and my wife's eternal lament, and my children's irrational demands. You'd be amazed how I had them all classified in my mind. I had my work classified like that. I don't even have the excuse that my job was particularly important to anyone other than myself. Not that it would have made much difference. Once you get into the routine of riding roughshod over love and affection, it takes major surgery before you can turn around. Somebody mentioned skill. I think that intimate personal relation is probably the rarest and finest skill of them all. I could never quite master it. And understanding, knowing about it, isn't enough."

Here the speaker seemed uncommonly moved suddenly and he excused himself. A few minutes later I caught sight of him in a far corner, by himself, smoking a cigarette. So I decided to risk an intrusion. I walked over to him and asked would he let me buy him a cup of coffee and would he rejoin us at the table. How relieved I was when he accepted! It was an awkward moment. But all of us at the table became a lot more talkative after that and some revealing things were said.

The girl to my right wanted it to be known that she was a single parent. "My biggest problem is being a friend and a parent at the same time," she confided. "One moment there is no intimacy. Then suddenly I have no authority. I question the quality of nearly everything I do, and half the time, when I should, I don't love my children. It's when I dislike them, I know, that's when I should love them, but more often than not, by the time that occurs to me, I've behaved stupidly or cruelly."

"Do you not suffer from depression?" I asked her. She said: "I do indeed. I don't believe that I myself was ever a teenager, can you accept that? A stage in my development is missing. That's how I diagnose my depression. Part of me wants to catch something up there and I won't let it. It's awful. Adolescence is the time for dreaming. All my dreams were knocked out of me by a critical education. Criticism was the plague even of my childhood. Everything and everyone was judged. You might say that the social milieu was judgment. I was desperately good at it myself. So good that after the age of fourteen I had no regard for anything. It's true that the sheer practise of criticism dries us up inside. I caught on to this when I was doing it to my own daughter, believe it or not. I began to listen to my own tone of voice. And I noticed the look in her eyes. I noticed how much I resented it that she should be able to experience something that was denied me, when I was her age. Whatever it was, I wanted to kill it off. It happened nearly automatically. I only had to give in to it."

"The essence of adolescence," somebody commented. "Has anyone ever defined it?"

Someone pointed to a poster on the wall advertising a performance of Miller's Crucible, by the local Drama Society.

"There you have an example of what can happen when adolescence is not only repressed but murdered outright," the man

33

in the yellow shirt suggested. "Multiple personality. Calvinism and Puritanism, what a team they make! How to take the joy out of life and demonstrate that you're too scared to miss it."

"Do you say that thwarted adolescence lay at the bottom of the Salem witch trials?" I wanted to know.

"Not at the bottom of the trials only, but of the accusations too," I was told. "During adolescence the spirit most explicitly – and exquisitely! – wants to become flesh. I'm convinced that we lay up a secret store of terrible afflictions for ourselves if we interfere with that process. We do so most commonly by refusing to come out of ourselves in terms of some creative activity – or by frustrating, or just plain neglecting, such creative activity in someone else, especially in our role as parents or teachers. Small wonder when suddenly the human psyche itself takes revenge, because it was never allowed to become a soul."

"It certainly must be a fundamental human impulse, that we show ourselves to the world, and our works to our fellow man. I see there the cause for the typical discontent of the housewife nowadays. It's not necessarily a vain conceit if we want others to know that we exist. The point is that we cannot ourselves live in the true sense unless we can give life to others. It has to be managed somehow or we feel that we fall by the wayside."

This from the banker. My heart sank. Suddenly for one reason or another I was conscious only of hypocrisy and criticism. I excused myself and left the cafeteria. I didn't want to make myself disagreeable to anyone, as I do invariably when I get depressed. Something was weighing on my mind. It wouldn't go away and I knew I would have to take some time to deal with it. So I decided on the walk around the lake. Perhaps I wouldn't even return to the debate. My brain was humming. The excitement of my own thoughts stirred my heart; how would I be able to take in what anyone else was thinking! Human character – it had to do with that. I was painfully aware of the stark contrast between my temperament at the moment and

the lake, the trees, the anglers half hidden in among the reeds –
all bathed in glorious sunshine, breathing contentment. My
mood vacillated between despair and aggression. It occurred to
me that a great deal had gone amiss with my own education.
What was wrong? Had I always followed the path of least re-
sistance? I called myself a teacher, and others called me a
teacher, but I lacked respect for myself. I followed the rules.
Probably no original thought had crossed my mind since I was
ten. The sum total of my skills amounted to a way with text-
books. I could answer a question if I could refer it to a book I
had read. My self-confidence began and ended with that. What
was to be done! Thirty-two years old, married, with two children, an urge to rebel and repeated bouts of self-disgust. My
poor wife! I had no use for her sympathy. She suffered because
she couldn't help me. And one's children sense it all too soon
when not everything is as it should be. And we should be
happy, shouldn't we! An unhappy person is either ill or bad,
that judgment had been drummed into me. Which was I then,
ill or bad? Probably a little of both.

So I decided to view myself in that light, as an individual
half ill and half bad, and therefore not happy. Perhaps never to
be happy. The best I could do was pretend. If no one guessed,
that was more than half the battle. I would continue to pretend
to be happy. But I was mean enough to refuse to be fooled by
this pretence myself. Henceforth my integrity would be based
on the secret knowledge that I was half ill and half bad. And I
would take pride in my expertise at convincing others of my
happiness. That would be my life skill. At school they were
beginning to teach some concoction called life-skills. Perhaps I
could put my name forward.

When I arrived back at the lecture hall they had started.

*

Geologist: . . . so I would always begin by finding out if the
pupil has something to say. I would give him every conceiv-

able opportunity to speak. It's no use lamenting the effects of television. Those are the pupils we've got and we may as well learn how to work with them.

Parent A: My daughter speaks a language of her own. I misunderstand every third thing she says to me. If I had some comparison, some notion of what a girl that age might be like if she had a perfect upbringing and education, then I could be guided. But there is no such model.

Parent B: That's right! We can't look at our children from the outside. How can we judge, when it comes to further education, whether or not they should carry on, or what subjects they should take? One minute you're afraid of pushing them into your own line of interest, the next minute you realize they have no interest at all, neither their own nor anyone else's. Our oldest daughter went into nursing. She has wanted to be a nurse since she was four. She has never wavered. We imagined that was normal. Along comes our second daughter. She is a profoundly unhappy girl. Exuberant and extroverted for two hours, then inconsolably depressed for the next two. She has no work habits. She goes to church twice a week; none of the rest of us go to church. I think I know more about outer space than I do about human nature. Can one in fact know anything about human nature? Maybe it's a case of one person at a time and everything else is fiction.

Philosopher: But the fiction is ever so important, don't you see. The fiction let's us formulate relations; we can manage associations and organize comparison. I would never look down on fiction. Our geologist relies entirely on illusion and appearance when he teaches, you heard him yourself. What I find outstanding is that he does so consciously and intentionally.

Sociologist: Let's keep in mind that further education is primarily not for children or pupils but for students who are young adults.

Parent C: let's not go down that path again.

36

Philosopher: But we must! We must! Otherwise we'll all throw our hands in the air and marvel at the miracle of our own situation and at the impossibility of doing or learning anything. We have to come to terms with reality.

The Banker: Surely that's commendable. But our society is fragmented. Our minds are adulterated. Our nature is promiscuous. A symposium like this can never come into the clear about anything unless we agree that something very special is required to make us see eye to eye, and that none of us can know ahead of time what that will be. If we're fortunate it will find us this afternoon. I would counsel a disposition of reverence. Wisdom comes to us when we are ready for it. It shuns logical dispute and traditional rationality. When we speak wisely we learn the truth. That sets us free.

A Student: I don't know whether to laugh or to feel ashamed of myself. Why is that? Here sits a man who tells us about our society, our minds, our nature. He must be wise. He says: 'our' minds are adulterated. Either he includes me, in which case I have a problem, because I don't really accept that my mind is adulterated, or he doesn't mean to include me but refers to some group to which he belongs, and in that case I wonder why he doesn't break loose and do something to chasten his mind. Or else he pontificates, uses the royal 'we', means all of us with our adulterated minds but secretly excludes himself as superior. In the light of that possibility I do get upset, because it amounts to him calling me names. He tells me my nature is promiscuous. Oh dear, I think to myself, that's terrible! What chance have I got! I feel so guilty! A promiscuous nature, an adulterated mind, not to mention my fragmented society! Pass me that revolver. Or that parcel of crack. Do you see what I mean? Mind you now, as I blow my brains out in the presence of his eternal sovereignty, let me do it with a disposition of reverence. Only then will I realize that 'the truth', not a bit of lead or a chemical substance, has set me free. – I hope you'll pardon

37

my outburst. I'm a student at this university and if I have learnt one thing it's to be suspicious of anyone who proposes that we speak wisely. What it usually means is: Let's all draw the conspiratorial curtain of hypocrisy over the proceedings. I haven't said a word since we started this morning because I figured, well, that I don't have much experience, especially in comparison to most of you here. But I've kept my ears open. Now it's time that I speak out. I want to make another thing clear: If I don't get put down now for being out of line or patronized for being young, then your so-called symposium will deserve the name.

The Banker: I apologize for what I said. It was said with the best intentions.

Student B: Oh, don't come with that. Good intentions! We know all about good intentions. Usually they end up getting us into trouble.

Student A: I accept your apology. But I think you should listen to how the prospect of further education appears to my own eyes, although I would not call myself a typical student. Typical students, so far as I can see, want to exploit the system, and far be it from me to fault them for it. The world is their oyster and they're ambitious to cultivate their pearls. It's not that I'm against the system, I just don't want to be part of it. But I will make use of it. In my opinion it's there to be made use of. My friends and I can argue endlessly about this. I mean about the difference between using a tool and identifying with it. This was my second year at University. I don't have the hang of it yet. There is not enough real personal contact between students and staff in terms of the so-called courses of study. Not for my liking. Or, more honestly, I myself can't make sufficient contact. Perhaps I have no right to suggest that it should be made simpler and easier for me. What I refuse to accept – and this is what makes me an atypical student, I believe – is that somewhere outside of myself and outside of my teachers and fellow students there exists a perfected and impersonal body of knowledge to which I can apply myself and with which I can identify in some useful way. Instead I believe that reality exists for each one of us only in direct proportion to the personal contribution we make to the experience that comes our way, whether inside or outside the classroom. Since we're mainly interested in education here I would limit the discussion to experience inside the classroom, or at least to what might be called the sphere of study.

A Parent: What course do you take, please?

Student A: Comparative literature, philology, that sort of thing. Let me tell you right away, there's no money in it, and I'll probably be teaching at a university myself some day. But not unless I can see my way clear to doing it in a way that shuts out idols, no matter how venerable they've become. My main worry is the sort of pseudo-heroic iconoclasm that gets rid of lesser idols to make room for bigger ones. I'd like to forget about idols altogether, whether they're ideas, or people, or whole fields of interest. I'd like to concentrate on my own development, on the cultivation of the two or three faculties I've discovered in myself so far. I look to the university for shelter while I exercise those faculties, for stimulation while I look for more, for understanding and spiritual companionship so that I'll have the confidence to risk learning to see and hear and touch in my own god-given way. And you know something? I sometimes suspect this university is not here for me at all, but that I'm supposed to be here for it. I'm tolerated. If I keep my nose clean I'm tolerated. I'm probably wrong about this, because I'm far too sensitive. On the other hand I'm far from the only one who has come to the conclusion that our university is not so much an institution for learning but a vehicle for propagating traditions and conventions; not so much a practice ground for spiritual skills as a transfer procedure for extinct data.

Philosopher: What, pray tell, do you mean by spiritual skills? I know what I would mean by it, but I'd certainly be interested in your version. Some people are frightened by the spirits. Others wallow in that business as though they had softened brains.

Student A: I believe that there is a spirit which informs us. All we have to do is ask for it. It also changes us. We want to do our best to cope with those changes. That's a skilful business, and one doesn't wallow in it. Also of course it's nothing to be afraid of.

Philosopher: So how do you cope with the changes due to that spirit? And how can it help you to involve yourself in formal education?

Student A: That's a good question. I'm hoping to find that out as I go along. I was told once, by a teacher at this university, that I'm not a student at all. I was interested in what that Geologist said earlier on about teaching illusion and appearance. That rang a bell. When I read a poem, for example, what interests me is precisely those spiritual skills that were employed by the poet. How can he show me, unless he avails himself of a few appearances and illusions? And, of course, the spirit is unique in that the skills one uses to cope with it are at one and the same time also the incorporation of that spirit. Spiritual skills are unique that way. That's why a comprehension of the skills that give us a certain poem do not necessarily help us write another poem, but they help us cope with the spirit then and there so that it becomes flesh in us. That's the life, then. That's what it's all about.

Geologist: That's intriguing. You and I could compare notes for a long time if we chose. We are discussing matters from a certain point of view here where art and science go hand in hand. I would love to relate this point of view to our notion of further education. We should be able to do this here. Anywhere else we'd be laughed at. This symposium is like a laboratory. Who knows what we'll discover.

Student A: I look forward to a time when equal amounts and degrees of art and science go into geology and poetry. Both of those terms, I mean art and science, will be somewhat redefined by then. Right now when you do geology you say you study the earth, little realizing perhaps (I don't mean you in person, by the way) how much you really study yourself and human nature in general, albeit in terms of this earth. Or you write a novel and you pile sentence on sentence while all the time you study the language you write in.

Geologist: You've missed the point surely. There's art in geology and science in poetry. It's as naïve to think of Geology as a mere look at the earth and its parts as it is to think of poetry as a mere construction of words. Both can be disciplines of the human spirit, first and foremost. Only those who have a very superficial insight only into the law of creation and creativity will wish to insist nowadays on an essential disparity between so-called physical nature, human nature and divine nature. Whatever is, surely, is worth studying. And the essence of being is humanity.

Theologian: If the essence of being is humanity, we waste our time analyzing appearances and interpreting illusions.

Geologist: Quite right, we do waste our time. But this is virgin territory. Our young friend here has introduced a vital element. We have cause to be grateful to him. The illusory, or apparent difference between the arts and the sciences is presented to young teenagers quite often as though ... well ... as though it somehow corresponded to a difference in themselves. But then we have to keep in mind that what is called arts and sciences now will probably not have that same name in a thousand years. I believe that even in this twentieth millennium still we undergo a transition of vast proportions. So while I would expect the retention of the terms art and science, I would not expect to see them in use as generic names for separate disciplines, but one and the same discipline will have both as distinct components. The art will refer to the practice and the science to the theory, something like that.

41

A Teacher: How futuristic is this? I mean should we take notes? Or are our feet still on the ground? This sounds like further and further education? Does it in fact matter whether the arts and the sciences are related?

Student A: It mattered a lot to me when I set out on my first university courses. I wanted to know exactly what I was letting myself in for. And I still do. If students can't ask these questions, who can? We should be able to look at everything as though for the first time. We should be encouraged to do so.

A Teacher: Your comments on art and science as one work went right past me. What kind of work do you envision for example in the realm of geology?

Geologist: I can only vaguely imagine it. The earth would not be seen as dead matter but as an organic entity, so that enquiries would be made not in the spirit of a search for a final explanation but for the sake of any number of lively impressions to stimulate a care-taking attitude, to kindle in the non-geological community a desire to cherish one's terrestrial environment; understanding of chemical and mechanical processes would aid the appreciation of the earth's beauty, its beauty as a machine, as an entirety within a greater one, as an apparently tailor-made home for mankind. Especially this particular notion would be emphasized, namely the earth as eminently suitable to mankind. Geologists and anthropologists would get together on this. One would not necessarily stop mining coal and drilling for oil, but there would be much less risk of an imbalance because these would be the lesser concerns in a much more comprehensive vision of the earth as something that can be forever known. Imagine a geologist who can write a paper on rock structure and can at the same time inspire us with a sense of wonder in the face of how marvellously these things are wrought. Of course he would have had to develop a visual organ for seeing that wonder in the first place.

Student A: And what about the poet now, in comparison. I dare say his prime ambition would not be a recollection of sentiment or a verbal expression of thought and emotion?

Geologist: No, exactly. His workshop would be those spiritual skills, scientifically understood and related. He would understand the spirit so that it can become flesh. His art would become much more communal than it is now, and he would help to create the collective myth that alone can gather a community, whether it's a global or a parochial community. Again you can see how science and art would between them make up the poetic work, just as they made up the geologic work. Poetry would not be an art any more than geology would be a science. Such disciplines as these would not be anything else, such as arts or sciences, because they would lead our faculties to the very edge of our horizon and back again, with no room to spare for walking around them and prescribing for them any limits. They would define their own limits, from within each discipline, and inherent to every work.

Student: Surely it would then be misleading and incorrect to call them all disciplines too.

Geologist: Well, strictly speaking, yes; I suppose. They would be what they are, at any given time. But that goes beyond our present scope, surely.

A Parent: Oh good! I'm glad that something does.

A Parent: I wonder. The least we can do is listen. Just because we can't comprehend something, that doesn't mean we have to dismiss it. On the contrary. I find myself touched by this. It sounds hopeful. Right now the world is divided into the top half that knows all the tricks and the bottom half that wants the treats, and the two halves don't meet very often, do they. The world is not a community but two camps. Everything is divided down the middle and from left to right. That's our collective cross. There is no common language. We talk at cross-purposes. We send or children to school so that they too will end up isolated.

Now here is someone who tells us that he believes it doesn't have to be like that, and that he can see a way out. I suppose the first thing we should do now is isolate <u>him</u>. Let's send him to Coventry, he challenged our closed minds.

Geologist: When I said that I like to teach appearance and illusion, well, I only wanted to indicate what my attitude was towards the outside world. Pupils, in a sense, come out of protective custody when they leave compulsory education. They are now not any more protected in that sense. They need rehabilitation. Otherwise the first thing they do is look for some other compulsory shelter, where their thoughts are thought for them and their feelings are felt for them. That's not life. My main theme therefore, within the context of further education, is the interpretation of our environment as the proper means to ourselves as spiritually robust and really healthy human beings. Oh, don't imagine that I would talk like this, I mean so openly, anywhere else. But further education, to me, is one bombshell of an idea. I never tire speculating about the possibilities; the endless possibilities. The outside world is appearance, the inside world is illusion. Let's not knock our heads against walls trying to prove it's different. The outside world is not the real world. The inside world is not the real world. But both those worlds together are the narrow road to reality. If it's reality and life we want, then we won't stop along the road somewhere as though we had arrived. Nor will we refuse to take to the road just because it's not in itself our destination. I teach Geology alright, but my end product is the humanity of my students. And here's another thing. I know that Geology is in one or another sense of the word a Science, and a discipline, with a sort of language all its own, but it has no life of its own. It moves whichever way we nudge it. So I maintain that a major concern of mine is the direction of the development of this science. The way I teach it determines how those who come after me will think and feel. It's a marvellous responsibility. It keeps me on the edge of my seat.

Philosopher: Ah well, good for you.

Geologist: Besides, I feel that any kind of a study should come up with results that make sense, potentially, to any- and every-body, not just to a select few. I don't mean to popularize it, but I dimly see a totally new direction, and a different thirst for knowledge too. Science is knowledge for the sake of under-standing. Understanding the earth means understanding it as a human earth, an earth for human beings, for beings who know the difference between a home and a house, between care and possessiveness, between love and greed. The idea therefore would be to recognize, realize and recollect the earth, to ac-knowledge wisdom in our being placed on this one, rather than on any other planet. One would consciously set out to collect evidence to prove beyond whatever contemporary doubt ex-isted that human nature and terrestrial nature dovetailed. One might make much of the geophysical parallel of gravity and aspiration. Climate and temperament would be compared, and once temperament is seen clearly, climate does not need to be contradicted. It falls into place. Gradually the superstition of one appearance causing another, or of an appearance causing an illusion, would wear thin. I trust I am losing my audience.

Sociologist: Sort of. Might you be raving?

Geologist: It feels like it sometimes. But I have my doubts. Take human character for example. The study of anything has to take human character into account, else it goes astray. Theol-ogy and astronomy can equally go astray like that, until even-tually they end up at each other's throats and one cannot with the best of wills take sides in the conflict. That's a veiled comment. – Look at it this way. My own character has to be continually put to the test – by myself. Unless I do it myself, it will be done for me. I consider, by the way, that the crucial dif-ference between the way the student learns and the way the pu-

45

pil goes about this is that the student increasingly puts <u>himself</u> to the test. Better expressed, he learns how to put his character to the test, and he gains character, and he learns how to use it. "Somebody has character" we say, and we view this largely as a passive state of being perhaps.

A Parent: And so it is, surely. It doesn't show up until there is conflict. Until we get into trouble.

Geologist: That's what I used to think. But that was before my student days. Then I discovered that it wasn't alright for me to sit down and wait, because everything was being taken care of for me, and in a way that required nothing from me except my passive compliance.

A Parent: So you couldn't wait. So you didn't have the patience. What kind of a student were you anyway?

Geologist: Well, you may have a point there. Mine may have been an exceptional case. But we learn from exceptional cases. That's what exceptional cases are for.

A Parent: No, I didn't mean that. I meant that maybe you just didn't have the patience to wait. When you go to school, especially to a university, don't you enter into a kind of contract? You say to the appropriate authorities: "Lay out your prepared program in front of me and I will try to respond to it as best I can."

Geologist: Ah well, initially yes. But I'm talking specifically about the nature of that response. I maintain that the student who waits to be spoon-fed is not a student at all, but less than a pupil. This is precisely where things can go wrong at the so-called institution of higher learning. The pupil, earlier in life, quite reasonably depends, to some extent and without knowing it, on the good will and initiative of his teacher. But as time goes on he should learn how to depend on his own resources. Not that the teacher withdraws his good will and initiative but that the student comes up with good will and initiative of is own. This transition, depending on the person, can be turbulent and problematic. It can also happen smoothly. But a fundamental transition is without question of the essence at this stage. Not that I would set myself up as a role model. Far from it. It seems to me, when I look back, that mine was one of the bumpiest transitions I've come across. But what it lacked in symmetry and harmony it made up for in terms of thoroughness. The difference between the individual and the universal was brought home to me rather emphatically. I often had to draw a sharp line between what only I myself could do and what was beyond me. And there was one thing I could do that made up for a whole lot, so to speak. While I worked away at that, most everything else tended to fall into place, of its own accord.

Philosopher: And what was that?

Geologist: I don't know that I had a name for it then, but today, in retrospect, I would call it self-critique. I think that may be a good name for it, although I may change my mind. I discovered that my own will as such wasn't much use to me. On the contrary, it got me into more trouble than enough.

Poet: Aha! Self-critique! I had imagined that only poets could know about self-critique. Evidently not.

Geologist: Well, as I said, I may find a better word for it. But it gave me something to do while I was waiting to be done to. One time I even thought I was done for, but I'll not go into that now. The point is that I was full of energy and animal spirits.

Poet: So what as wrong with that?

Geologist: Oh nothing at first. I had a great time. I played football, I went on expeditions, in the States that was, I lived in California at the time, my parents were civil servants - but then something put a stop to that.

Poet: Something?

Geologist: It occurred to me that I was wasting my time. So I decided to go back to school. Then I really got into trouble. I didn't want to toe the line. Unfortunately the university I went to was more like a kindergarten. Their ambition was to turn out predictable, standard technicians. My own ambition was to make contact with a source of life, wherever that was. I did not very often see eye to eye with my teachers. Not until I decided to fake it. That may be too strong a term. But I honestly felt that if I wanted to be educated I should go full steam ahead and not let a handful of ungifted, so-called teachers stand in my way. So I learned to pretend. Privately I studied whatever it was that forced itself on me at the time – I suffered a lot of depression – and publicly I tried as best I could to please my instructors. I led a double life. I wish it hadn't been necessary. I could have used a lot of help that I didn't get; the sort of help that I try to give my own students today.

Poet: But how can you help a person do what only he himself can do?

Geologist: Yes, that's the burning question. That's where the self-critique comes in. First of all, if you're a teacher, you can stop sounding as though you knew it all and as though it were possible for you to supply the student with all he needed to be a success, if only he does what he's told. That's the thing not to do. It means foregoing the pleasure of a lot of self-congratulatory rhetoric. If you want to hold forth, you should go into politics. Equally, on the negative side, is the assumption by the teacher that he really can't do anything except present some material, some data, some textbook-rehash, and it's up to the student how much he takes in and regurgitates during exam time or on term papers. On the much more important, positive side, the teacher can practice self-critique himself. In that way he sets the example for what he dearly wishes the student would do too. He sets the example for something that can only be transmitted by example. When it works, the results are remarkable and often startling. While it doesn't work, the teacher keeps doing it all the same because he knows that on one hand it's the best he can do, and on the other hand it's equally profitable for him as a productive individual, whether anyone follows his example or not.

Poet: But can he not talk <u>about</u> self-critique? Can it not be taught, as a skill in itself?

Geologist: No it can't. It has to be transmitted, by example. Once a student catches on, well, it's like a secret between the teacher and the student, a note of mutual respect, a tacit understanding of where the shoe pinches when it does pinch, of the fact that the wind blows when it does blow. It means that one puts oneself to the test. One acknowledges that as an individual one does not have all it takes and nevertheless one tries for perfect. One insists on the value of one's humanity in spite of a shortage of suitable definitions. And one doesn't wait for anybody's approval, that's crucial; least of all for the approval of parents, teachers and friends, because what they are interested in usually is the finished product and not the process. Your best friend will be the one who tells you: Don't talk bout it; do it.

Poet: I'm still not much the wiser. Are we trying to talk about what can't be talked about? If so, why did you mention it in the first place?

Philosopher: Perhaps we should recap. We agreed there might be some sense in looking at further education as a development of spiritual skills and a building up of character. Then our geologist friend said that he teaches by means of appearances and illusions, which surprised us a little, but I think we know what he means now. What we have trouble with is his definition of self-critique. To me personally it does in fact sound like another skill, but a skill that is directed inward, away from illusions and appearances. It's not even correct to say 'inward', really, because we've decorated the 'inward' aspect with illusions already, in counter-distinction to the outer aspect, which we ornamented with appearances. So the self-critical skill …

Geologist: No! Hold it there! There is nothing self-critical or critical in any other sense about it. I must be adamant about

49

that. Self-critique is not self-criticism. Mind you, I can see now what you mean when you call it another skill. In our own sense now, it would really be the skill that precedes all other skills. But it has nothing to do with appearances or illusions.

Philosopher: then what does it have to do with? Surely not with reality per se!

Poet: You do call them spiritual skills, don't you? In other words, none of them, whether intellectual, intuitive, instinctive or intelligent, are willed individually, but they all stem from our reliance on spirit, that is to say: reality. Nobody could boast of a spiritual skill because in the absence of reality such skills are not operative, are they. The spirit is not in our power, after all, is it. We have the power of the spirit, but only while the spirit wills, not we ourselves. Except of course for our initial leaning in the direction of those skills. On that score you might say that we're on our own entirely. Is that maybe where you want to come in with your self-critique? Because let's face it, our self may have put on a fair show of its own before we catch on to it. And then we have to come to terms with that, don't we. Poets repent too. Sometimes we repent halfway into every poem. We shake off the self in favour of the spirit. Then the spirit returns us to ourselves, all in one piece, I might add.

A Parent: Marvellous! That's what I was looking for! Now I can see the head and the tail of it.

A Teacher: Yes. Now I can relate all this to my own experience. Self-critique: You mean the job we can do ferreting out our complacency at a time when we don't feel particularly down-hearted. Or the way we can say: Yes, now I'm happy, now let me bend down to some unhappy person, and look how disinclined I am to do that – for shame!

A Scientist: Or the way we can at any moment of the day suddenly say to ourselves: Let me look to my god now – and we notice how the revulsion boils up in us. Let me turn to the Christ of my religion – and the resentment clouds our eyes.

50

And then we have this revulsion and this resentment on our hands and we have all the opportunity in the world for doing something with them, because that's where all our gifts and talents are rooted, so far as I know.

Student B: Good heavens!

Geologist: I would never have imagined that we would go the full distance, but we have done. We entered the sphere of the gifted student. What a pleasure, what a tremendous satisfaction, for a teacher, when that happens in his presence! Some young hopeful individual has been slogging away patiently for half a year when suddenly he is touched by the human spark. Doors open in his mind where he didn't even know there were walls. He branches out. He writes with flair. There's a spring in his step.

A Teacher: Did that happen to you when you were a student?

Geologist: Yes it did. And I remember it very well. I was quite shocked by it all. I found that I suddenly had authority. I say 'suddenly', but I mean more or less over a period of half a year or so, when it dawned on me that I was on the right track. The authority brought a special responsibility along with it, and I balked at that for a while. I have since discovered that most serious students come up against that problem in one form or another. One has to forgive them certain unbearable airs of omniscience at times.

Student A: I'm still not happy about your definition of human character. I regard myself as a serious student while I attend university, and I think I know what you mean by authority and the need for responsibility, although I'm not very far into that yet. What worries me is a kind of moral light-headedness that besets me at times. It's a debilitating condition. I feel ever so full of myself, on top of the world, a bit impatient of all the slowpokes to my left and right, and sometimes downright contemptuous of the human race as a whole, and all on account of all the things I can allegedly do. What worries me most is that when that condition grows on me, I gather hangers-on. They

51

encourage me in that state. Happily it's not long before I get my come-uppance then, although at the time I don't necessarily agree that this is good for me, and more often than not I despair all over again of ever being able to amount to anything on God's earth. It's difficult for me to keep my feet on the ground, in touch with gravity, and a solid foundation underneath. All too often I rise up away from the ground or I sink down into it. Does that make sense to you?

Geologist: I believe I'm familiar with it a little bit. The fact that you recognize it, that you even have a name for it, seems very hopeful to me. 'Moral light-headedness' may very well be quite apt. It invites a definition of morality as the state of being at ease within mortal bounds. How we acquire that state is another question. You're at the right age for tackling such a problem. If you solve it, for yourself and in your own way, a lot of people will have reason to be thankful to you for it. As for human character, the way I see it – certainly that touches on morality. It more than touches on it.

Student B: I think I should say at this point that I really can't take all this very seriously. Can I be totally honest? Where school is concerned, especially since I made the doubtful decision to go on with my education, I am most of the time in a fog. In fact I'm hoping to get rid of that fog if I keep going to school, but so far it only continues to thicken. Schoolwork is still one chore after the other. When it comes to writing your typical school essay I can't think of anything to say, and that's putting it mildly. As soon as somebody puts pressure on me I get sullen and resentful and that puts up even more of a barrier for me. If somebody eere to give me a good reason for quitting, I would. So far I've only heard reasons for going on. Progress, in my personal environment, is identified with A levels and a university degree. My brother is a genius at it. My sister can't wait to go to school. It makes me feel inadequate. I cannot fathom what you people mean by spiritual skills. Or by character. Of by a taste for reality. All that stupefies me. I hear the sound of those words and my brain makes a funny sort of a rushing sound that blocks out my hearing and clouds my sight. It happens at school too. A teacher comes in and starts to talk about calculus. Or poetry, it doesn't matter which. I make a genuine effort to take it all in, to sort it, to control it, to memorise it so that I've got it in front of me and so that I can answer questions about it, but after five minutes or so I'm sitting by myself on a small island surrounded by stormy sea. Five minutes later I could hardly tell you what my name was, and that teacher's voice is a monotonous drone. Within ten minutes I've turned into an idiot. I mean it. I feel like an idiot. Now what about further education? Has formal education turned me into an idiot and will further education turn me more thoroughly into an idiot? Maybe I'm on the wrong track altogether, when I have hopes that at school I'll gain some understanding; a little clarity about myself. I don't understand myself, don't you see? You can talk all day about calculus and population movements and objective art criticism and the chemical properties of soapstone but who is this lump right here, this thing that parades up and down in my skin or takes up space in a chair! That's what I need to know. I think I resent being told in such detail who a whole lot of other people are, such as Macbeth and Freud and Napoleon, when I feel such an absolute stranger to myself. But perhaps I'm nobody. That scares me a bit. Perhaps there's nothing there. Nor ever will be. But I doubt that. If that were the case, why would I be so concerned? Prince Nobody doesn't worry. He's a contented cog in the system.

Psychologist: Now here we have a puzzling situation. It sounds to me like you're a glutton for punishment. Imagine volunteering to be made a feel like an idiot!

A Parent: That's hardly fair. He did say he had hopes of being educated out of it.

Philosopher: But if the education brings it on in the first place, how can ...

A Parent: We have talked about this. The student pits himself against the curriculum and then deals with the organic response in himself.

Geologist: Quite right. That fog. Do you know what I would call it? The object matter. The subject matter of the curriculum sets off the object matter of the psyche. In this present case the reaction is so strong as to be nearly overwhelming. Why not call it your idiocy and be done with it. Think of it as a familiar friend and learn how to behave in his company. My guess is that you won't have long to wait before he starts to respond to your overtures of friendship. But you have to believe that he's there for your benefit. If you struggle against it as though it intended to get in your way, you will merely exhaust yourself. The believing is important. Not every one of us knows how to believe, intentionally and physically. We confuse believing with just not questioning. We go through life in doubt of just about everything and then when for a moment we suspend our doubt, we call that believing. But refusing to break eggs is not the same as making an omelette. I would say that an element of doubt is in fact required if we really want to get down to the concrete business of believing. And if you set about believing that objective reaction, that psychic output which I called object matter, you are actually working. That's what it means to work, as a serious student. I have no doubts about that whatsoever.

Student B: Usually I think of work as a case of digging into myself. Sheer will-power.

Geologist: That's not work. That's self-sacrifice. It's less than useless. It's damaging. You should have had that explained to you by now. It's one of my quarrels with the education system, that work is just not explained. It isn't properly taught, I mean the physiology of it. Instead we praise breathless and fruitless labour and even more we applaud what you just described, that self-punishing intensity towards some dead end. Work should intrigue us, instil in us a sense of wonder; then we pay that back; we plough it back into the process. Secretly I envy you. I wish I had your problem. If you but knew it, you're coming down with useful goods. You have so much of a crop that you don't know how to start harvesting. But I do hope you start soon. It will change your life, even while you're still at school.

Student B: Thank you for your concern. I wish I could see it your way.

Geologist: No reason why you can't. Wait until you feel normal. It's bound to happen sooner or later, if only for a few minutes. Then say to yourself: Where does this stupor come from, when it does come? It must come from somewhere. Nobody is put on the rack for no reason. Then keep a close lookout for when it starts. Decide that it shows up as somehow separate from you, this idiocy of yours. Alright? You want one thing, it wants another, isn't that so? If it's slow in arriving, especially while you watch for it, tackle some job. Pick something you've put off for a while. You'll probably only have to think of it, of that essay on Hamlet, for the shades to come down. Right, you didn't miss it that time. You caught it at the beginning. It's a great big sense of failure and despair this time. Or something like it. You don't need to name it, or to describe it; only to identify it and then to say: I believe this. That's human character at work. Believe that pressure that forces itself into you, and know that it's the best part of you. Know that it's the part of you that we all have in common, if we but knew it. Know that it's our human being and then believe that human being. This business of believing appears to be the tricky bit for some of us. It helps if you can pretend to yourself that you're a total youngster, without hang-ups, right up front with your emotions and not afraid to trust. Your human being is the one that comes out in response to efforts, due to your application.

And then you would get around it! Imagine that! The best part of you! You would repress it, so that you can get on with what you planned. What your human being wants, contrary to you who want to write an essay on Hamlet, is to become you. It wants to be you. Believe it and let it become you. That absorbs it, like a fish absorbs water. You assimilate it then, due to your believing. Believe that it works while you do it, and understand, if you can, that your human being knows better. Really it wants to be your essay. And you would suppress it so that you can write your essay! No wonder you hate yourself. That human being of yours came forward as soon as you made your intentions clear. It didn't come out from within you and it didn't enter you from outside, just suddenly it's there. But this time you expected it, didn't you; because I told you to expect it. So you weren't bowled over by it. You weren't frightened. You didn't get paralytic. The son of man, your human being, is the very best part of you. Don't betray him. Believe in him.

Young Man: Now you've looked at human character from a different angel, surely. I don't see any opportunity at all for testing or for self-critique.

Geologist: No, quite right. Not as soon as you believe. Not when all this raw-material is available for believing. Not when somebody is so intelligently aware of his 'idiocy'. But we shouldn't forget that most students are not at all articulately aware of what goes on within themselves. They may be in a mood, but even if they don't necessarily indulge themselves in that mood, they still don't realize they are in a mood. They pass from one state of being to another without realizing that and of course without recognizing any of those states. In other words their real education is nil. And character they have none. I mention the extreme because one should come to terms with the fact that to all external intents and purposes an individual can function brilliantly, at school too, and be totally devoid of character and the benefits of education. Such an individual has

56

managed to arrive at a relatively early age at a state of what I call extinction. He has managed it himself, because you couldn't do that to anybody against his will, but he has also been 'managed' in that direction, by those who are part of the system.

A Teacher: And obviously you can't fault the system for that.

Philosopher: Of course one can, but it doesn't do any good. Even if one were right it wouldn't do any good.

A Parent: So here we have someone now called the extinct student. Marvellous! I wonder, does he know about it?

Psychologist: Of course not. Presumably he succeeds and is proud of himself. And woe to him who tries to disabuse him. The extinct student is on top of the world. He wins the awards. Not all of them, but a goodly number. If you were to challenge him in the pursuit of his career he would quietly ask you to keep out of his way.

Student A: But he has no character, am I right?

Geologist: None.

Student B : Because he finds himself in a cause and effect relationship with appearances and illusions as though they were realities, am I right? He learns the lingo of illusions and becomes an illusion; he learns the patter of appearances and becomes an appearance. Is that what it means to be part of the world, I wonder?

Young Person: Surely that's one way of looking at it. The arts and sciences are so many adventures of the human spirit. The list is endless. But there's one supreme adventure, when that human spirit gets to know itself. It reflects on itself and sees there the reality of everything. Then it rejects the arts and sciences as approximations. But it doesn't make a thing out of that rejection. It avoids nihilism and mysticism. Instead it sets itself up as a teacher. It says: I have found the solution to all the ills of the earth and the troubles of mankind. Let me show you how it's done. Then the students arrive and they say: Go ahead,

57

show us! – Ah! says our friend, the teacher: The first thing to do is work on your senses. You have not yet learned how to see. Your vision is faulty. Therefore I recommend to you that you find some activity that will exercise your vision. Such as writing poetry, or painting images. But always make sure that you think about what you do while you do it. Gradually you will make progress. You will learn how to see and hear in many different ways. You will discover the physical and organic difference between gazing and looking, between insight and observation, and above all you will be glad to admit that all these skills can be improved and perfected, and that the world changes continually in accordance with your changing skills. That will be a sobering thought. You won't be in quite such a rush now to change the world, when you notice how it likes to change continually by itself, to amuse you and to keep you guessing.

Student B: "And what's the next thing, please?" asks the student, after he has some of these skills down pat.

Young Person: The next thing is to project your spirit into the universe, for the sake of mankind.

Student B: "Good grief, how do I do that?" says the student.

Young Person: You actively engage in the process of reproducing yourself – the teacher suggests. You show yourself in this light today and in that light tomorrow. Then you show yourself from below, from above, from the inside and from the outside. The perfected skills of your senses are your new body. You have a real body of knowledge now, and whoever sees it, or comes into contact with it, will definitely feel urged to try to acquire one himself. We all want live knowledge. And we don't want the promise of it, as made by the arts and sciences which won't admit until they're fatigued that they can't keep that promise, but we want the real thing. – That's how I see education and further education, in a nutshell.

A Mother: And morality?

58

Young Person: How can anyone who has live knowledge behave in any other than in a perfectly suitable way? Morality is that system of good customs and habits that rests – not on little pleasures and pains, but on a healthy body in reality. A live body of knowledge is really nothing to be scoffed at. When you feel the truth you don't steal from your neighbour or play tricks on your spouse. When you see the light you don't tell lies to deceive your friends or to subject your enemies to harm. Of course there are those who mistakenly assume they can gain happiness by leading a moral life, but that generation is with us for a comparison. No, first comes the happiness, the blessedness of the human spirit content in its own company, and then morality is the automatic outcome. Who could sin if he could see straight and clear!

Student A: Yes, especially if you define sin as the unwillingness or failure to see straight and clear. I'll tell you one thing, we won't make any converts with that line of reasoning.

A Father: I think it's too late for making converts in any case. Whoever hasn't got the picture nowadays is too busy fabricating his own to be open to persuasion. Clubs get more club members, that's true and popular schemes have their hangers-on, and there are more than enough organizations and ideologies and –isms squabbling over the 'single people', who doesn't exist in any case, since only human beings, not people, come one at a time. But then all through our comments on further education runs this thread of a double standard, doesn't it. It certainly seems that way to me. Yes, a double standard. Some can be educated and some cannot. But one has to put a good face on it. So one can't make do with one single definition of education. One has to have two. There is one with a capital E and one with a small. The big Education is for the dolts who want to be right. The small education is for those who know that they're invariably in the wrong, and they need to be educated to be able to accept that truth gratefully – I mean grace-

fully. Really I mean both. Everybody knows, or at least sus-
pects, that we have a choice of masters. So why shouldn't there
be a choice of two educations? Right through from playschool
to the Doctorate of Philosophy, whatever that means.

A Teacher: A day will come when outbursts like that will be
judged to be so unreasonable as to be treasonable. I'm not
speaking about State control, but mind control. There is something like treason against the mind. If a person understands
something, he has to take into account that those who don't understand are not all necessarily evil – in the same way as he
cannot take all the credit himself for his understanding. Others
have laboured. Others have strained to push the cart of individual intelligence up the communal hill. So let's not have any of
this defeatist nonsense about the final decision having been
made. If it had been made, we would surely all know about it.

A Father: Not necessarily. The guest of honour has gone home
but the rest still dance and sing and carry on because their
minds are too foggy to have noticed.

The Teacher: I give up

Philosopher: Don't' give up. We are not primarily looking for
harmony and agreement, are we? Let's recognize the effective
validity of a genuine dispute.

The Banker: In my opinion we are in total disarray.

Poet: So what. That's nothing to be sad about. I wish I had a
pound for every time that has happened to me in my work. The
seed-corn has to die. Let's come up with the courage to wait
for the new crop. Let's assist one another. We don't even have
to say anything. In a sense we have arrived at a position, col-
lectively, that should be familiar to most adolescents, or to anybody who thinks he can plan out his life. An act of the popular
will does violence to life, so I suggest we resign ourselves to
rejecting that option. Let the proprieties be served at a time when
nothing else serves. Our pronouncements at the best of times
are approximations, so why not indulge in a few moments of

total honesty. It can only do us good. This symposium is going through something like an initiation at the moment. I recognize it. To me that's a guarantee that up to now we have not been wasting our time.

A Parent: Tell us about your activity as a poet.

Poet: My own personal activity? I study the spirit of god in the minutest detail. And I report on my findings in the English language. That's really all there is to it. I have sometimes wondered why I write poems rather than novels, but I can only imagine that it's a matter of temperament. For me, temperament is the most interesting part of human nature.

A Teacher: Would you recite one of your poems?

Poet: Tell them they have their world disguised
          as principles, as finite dreams
          that cannot – will not be realized,
          so as a consequence it seems

          there must be this glorious upheaval,
          frankly in aid of the dance
          for the sake of our life's retrieval
          From the stones, the beasts and the plants.

A Parent: I don't understand. Who are 'they'? and who are 'we'? And who speaks?

Poet: There you put your finger on the value of poetry as a means towards further education. It has to be poetry that springs from human being and from the spirit

Philosopher: Please explain.

A Parent: No, I really don't think we should get into that now. Poetry is a form of entertainment. What does entertainment have to do with education?

Poet: There is a poetry that is basically entertainment, and I don't despise it. When we're happy and full of life, entertainment is very important to us. Without it, happiness becomes selfish and we become inconsiderate and intolerant of others.

Our culture largely has to do with entertainment, in the widest and in the narrowest sense. That's my opinion, anyway. Take it or leave it.

Geologist: But then how do you see poetry as conducive to further education?

Poet: Well, until now we've only looked at further education from the point of view of voluntary versus compulsory education. It still remains for us to familiarize ourselves with it entirely on its own grounds. "Further" in that case would mean more or less ongoing, rather than "beyond compulsory". There are students who insist on that meaning very early in life. I mean: very early in their life as students. For them the creative element, something I would call enlightenment, moves to the forefront. That element was introduced a little while ago by a student – that young man there. Can you recall what you said? You said you believed that there was a spirit which informs us, and that all we have to do is ask for it. You also mentioned 'the poet'. I didn't speak up at the time but I listened to what you said. I found it interesting that a teacher told you he didn't think of you as a student at all. You referred to poetry as first and foremost an example of spiritual skill. Do I remember correctly?

Student A: I don't actually, no, I'm sorry. I can't recall what I said but I'm sure you're right.

Poet: Certainly I write some poetry as entertainment. Sometimes I can't help myself. But somehow I don't believe that is what's needed nowadays. There's no shortage of the kind of entertainment that helps us forget ourselves – and everything else for that matter. It's a reaction to animal spirits, I think. I don't agree with it because in my opinion our so-called animal spirits are valid enough just so long as we transform them and they don't transcend us. I don't deny there are emergencies when the quick escape is expedient, but drugs as a way of life are bound to turn us into cretins and zombies. When I speak of poetry as entertainment, therefore, I assume, as given, a surfeit of real life, not a bout of nervous energy. So prior to poetry as that kind of life-furthering entertainment, we need the poetry that builds and constructs for life.

Philosopher: Am I correct in assuming that philosophy would do instead of poetry?

Poet: Philosophy from you, perhaps, but not from me. If I called it reborn genius nobody would believe me. But whether it's poetry, or philosophy or geology, as we decided some time ago, what counts is the individual human source and the personal example.

Geologist: Right. Now get back to your use of poetry for further education.

Poet: Yes, as I said, I'd like us to discuss further education not in comparison and contrast to compulsory education now, but on its own grounds, as a distinct desire, and in particular as the desire to please God. I would call that a fundamental desire, and very nearly akin to what we usually mean by wanting to be ourselves, by wanting to be who we are, by finding ourselves. We may not be happy with a great deal in our lives, our conditions strike us as being arbitrarily imposed, even the thoughts we think and the feelings we feel occur to us as really and truly someone else's property, and we only borrowed it, or it was lent to us with the best of wills, but here suddenly now we seem capable of something that would be characteristically our own but we cannot find the space or the time, mental or physical, to develop and offer it up. So we're stymied.

Sociologist: I have to agree that the desire to be oneself is usually strongest in those who have had their nature overlaid for some time by spiritual baggage. You come across this rather graphically in the case of the so-called 'social dropout'. He retires from the rat race so that he can take the time to assess his injuries and maybe join the human race instead.

Psychologist: There's the group person, and the tradition person. Both of them have a hard time of it if that particular desire makes itself felt in their case and …

Poet: Ah, but let's not get into the general malaise of the misfit here. The thirst for education rarely hits those who have lived in the past for forty years, or under the umbrella of some spurious ideology. If this is going to make sense right now we'll have to limit ourselves to the young person. I mean specifically the student who has left the pupil behind and finds himself motivated quite independently. He looks to the future with courage, and when he reflects on that courage he recognizes it, not as something trumped up but substantial. If he sees it as the desire to please god he knows he has to look no further than that desire in order to come to terms with god. If he feels that he needs to 'find himself', why then he searches within the confines of that need and guards himself against popular determinations from outside it.

A Parent: And the poetry?

Poet: Ah well, let's say he wants to coordinate the data he has picked up during the past fifteen years. Let's say he's coming down with information from all his previous education and he can't make head or tail of it. Thousands of so-called facts clutter up his brain. That's a tremendous burden for someone who is suddenly supposed to stand on his own two feet. It's a burden even for someone who knows that one day he will have to stand on his own two feet. The facts have been funnelled into him, most of them were indigestible on account of being extinct material, dead explanations for inane queries, all quite respectable and above board of course in the conventional light. He searches for the missing link. Of course there is no such thing, but that's where poetry comes in, ideally suited for creating order out of chaos, one might say. I hope it doesn't need to be said again, but I don't mean sentimental rhymes. I mean a vehicle for the creative spirit. That spirit is creative because it wants to create me and you, and it turns all those facts into useful illusions towards a greater end.

Student B: What in heaven's name does it mean to be created, then, since we're into meaning? I thought we have all been created, as a species, years ago.

Philosopher: Excellent question!

Poet: It pleases God immensely that we should want to be created by him. The more we please God, the more we become ourselves. To be created means to become who we are. God's pleasure is our becoming. Why are we here in the first place? Not to activate the universe on our behalf, that's for sure. Surely there are a lot of us who desire that God should exist. That's the same desire as that I should become who I am. Self-realization is no grandiose pact with the devil. Don't let it become a cult-concept either. Your self-motivated student sees in poetry a natural way forward. He doesn't mind climbing hills now because he recognizes the direction and he has the scent of the goal. To be created means to be changed in favour of the truth. We can't change ourselves, that may be a bitter pill to swallow for a naturally active and ambitious individual, but that only means that his activity and ambition need to be redirected – by him. The fact that I am not the agent of my change, this implies that I'm the agent for conditions that favour my change. To praise and to adore god, scientifically speaking, this is the agency for those conditions. But don't forget that God years ago became human. You need the memory of an elephant for that. Human being is God's proper domain now. The human soul is his playground. The independent student will learn not to be afraid of that. Let's say that the study of poetry will fill some of his spare time. Whatever else he does then benefits from that acquired sense of perspective. He won't mistake appearances and illusions for reality after a while – to borrow a notion from our geologist. He'll return to his creative self for sustenance.

Philosopher: So further education all of a sudden contains that kernel of self-sufficiency, does it? I don't see much justice in that. It's because I don't have much faith in the self.

Poet: Now you're on a different track altogether. I said nothing about 'the self'. That's a monstrosity, I know. It's the myth that befogs our best minds. Let's instead cling to the idea of further education as self-motivated. The student needs to go no further than his own desire in order to be motivated, and in order to be motivated towards anything he studies. His character is established, so that he can rely on that desire as sober and temperate. First came the critique that established his character. Then comes the desire, and always in a version he can trust. He will trust it, let's put it that way. We are not in the presence now of an individual whose singularity we respect; that was the case while the student distanced himself from the pupil. We are now in the company of a person whose presence we honour. You don't lecture a person like that. You exchange thought and feeling with him. You let him realize your ideas and you realize his. But before he enters that phase of his development he has to make his own – to appropriate – some vehicle for the creative spirit.

Young Man: Such as poetry.

Poet: In my own case, poetry. What we want is that there should be as many such vehicles available to the student as possible. Mathematics for example. But again it has to be said that for mathematics to be a vehicle for spiritual transformation – i.e. for further education – it has to be handled in a slightly different fashion from what one sees today.

A Parent: Our conversation has headed in that direction right from the start, so it seems to me. As our notion of further education has developed, so has the need arisen to reappraise the use we make of academic disciplines, and even those disciplines themselves are now open to question.

A Teacher: That's what a symposium like this is for. It should be possible to ask any and every question, and to try a great variety of answers, without being overly concerned about practical feasibility or likelihood. One way to change worn-out attitudes is to challenge them directly.

Young Man: So you do believe that mathematics could become the kind of total-environment discipline that a student requires if his .. what did we call it ... his desire to please god – or to become who he is – should bear fruit?

Poet: Let's put it this way: If mathematics does not become such a discipline, what earthly use it? The modern spirit, during the past twenty centuries, has taken us to the point of extinction. There are still a few loose ends to tie up, but by and large you might say the globe has arrived. The nations have had their innings, and some of them had a good one.

Sociologist: How can you call the point of extinction an arrival? Surely what we usually mean by an expression like that is a dead end!

Poet: Everybody has to arrive at it sooner or later. For some, the trip was a bit more orderly than for others. But nobody on the earth's surface could avoid that stage on the way to knowledge or annihilation. I guess I contribute my efforts to those for whom this dead end means a new beginning. I really can't speak for the rest. But why shouldn't there be a new beginning in terms of mathematics? Call it mind-measurement. – or in terms of physics, for that matter. Of course if you still belong to that mild-mannered remnant of the tribe who want to do things like 'split the atom' and explode the globe to kingdom come, then ... well ... you are one of those little ends that still need to be tied up. You may be in the numeric majority for all I care, you are nevertheless, in the face of reality, a dwindling remnant.

Student B: So can you give us some idea of the mathematics you envision?

Poet: I will have a go at envisioning it right now on the spot, if you like, but I can't guarantee that anything I come up with will appeal to anyone. Not that I haven't given it some thought; a poet holds himself responsible for a familiarity with everything under the sun. I see mathematics as the study of name and number, in relation to each other and each to itself. There is a number that has the name five. When we talk about five horses we relate that number to something outside itself or its name, namely horses, so we can say that counting has nothing to do with mathematics. That limits the field. But if we study five, not five this or five that, just five, we come up with all sorts of interesting speculations, and their purpose would be to enliven our mind, to put us in the possession of our mind for one thing; after all, that mind is not necessarily yet _our_ mind. What I mean by mind-measuring brings that about, so that mathematics in general could be defined as the appropriation of the mind. The mind, which is mythic, becomes _our_ mind, which is organic, due to our mathematical pursuits. When we name something, now, we extend to it some part of ourselves. Horse is a name. That extension can only be managed by someone in the possession of his mind, because then it's a true name otherwise it's a label. Most people only ever deal in labels. To those with no mind of their own even horse is a label. When we begin to reflect on horse as a name we come up with a great variety of suggestions which make our life colourful. Technically we are involved in a meeting of minds. So the secondary purpose of mathematics is to render appearance and illusion more various and manifold for ourselves and others. The primary purpose, that we have our own minds, is a prerequisite for this. When two or three of us who are in the possession of our own mind come together we can then be of one mind, which is truly marvellous and well worth looking forward to and setting up for. People with no mind of their own can't possibly be of one mind. – what we call something, this has nothing to do with mathematics. Naming and numbering are in, counting and calling are out. And so on and so forth. Once we get into this business with a whole heart and a sound mind, one thing soon leads to another and before we know it we have a perfect body of knowledge. Then others can make use of that to acquire their own. Your own mind in a body of knowledge is a wonderful example to the world and mankind.

Philosopher: Well now, that's taking further education about as far as it will go.

Scientist: To the point where it becomes endless, I should think.

* * * * *

www.ingramcontent.com/pod-product-compliance
Lightning Source LLC
Chambersburg PA
CBHW070312290526
45791CB00003B/1105